★ ★ ★

B-52
STRATOFORTRESSES

BY JACK DAVID

BELLWETHER MEDIA · MINNEAPOLIS, MN

Are you ready to take it to the extreme?
Torque books thrust you into the action-packed
world of sports, vehicles, and adventure. These books
may include dirt, smoke, fire, and dangerous stunts.
WARNING: read at your own risk.

Library of Congress Cataloging-in-Publication Data

David, Jack, 1968-
  B-52 Stratofortresses / by Jack David.
      p. cm. – (Torque. Military machines)
  Includes bibliographical references and index.
  Summary: "Amazing photography and engaging information explain the technologies and
capabilities of the B-52 Stratofortress. Intended for students in grades 3 through 7"–Provided by
publisher.
  ISBN-13: 978-1-60014-259-8 (hbk. : alk. paper)
  ISBN-10: 1-60014-259-1 (hbk. : alk. paper)
  1. B-52 bomber–Juvenile literature. I. Title.

  UG1242.B6D377 2009
  623.74'63–dc22   2008035310

This edition first published in 2009 by Bellwether Media, Inc.

The photographs in this book are reproduced through the courtesy of the United States Department
of Defense.

Printed in the United States of America.

CONTENTS

THE B-52 IN ACTION

More than 8 miles (13 kilometers) above ground, a single B-52 Stratofortress cruises through the clouds. The B-52's crew has its target, a terrorist camp, in sight. The enemy on the ground is unaware the B-52 is flying overhead.

The **commander** gives the order to drop a bomb. The plane's bomb bay opens and releases a **laser-guided bomb (LGB)**. The bomb locks onto the target as it speeds down toward the ground. The terrorist camp explodes as the bomb strikes.

The crew confirms the hit on **radar**.
Then they start the long flight home to
their base. Their **mission** is a success.

LONG-RANGE HEAVY BOMBER

The B-52 is a long-range heavy bomber. It can fly missions halfway around the world at very high **altitudes**. It can drop almost any type of bomb the United States Air Force uses. The B-52 has been in U.S. Air Force service since 1954.

During the Gulf War, B-52s flew the longest mission in history. They made a 35-hour, 16,000-mile (26,000-kilometer) round trip from Louisiana to the Persian Gulf.

The Air Force has made many changes and additions to the B-52 since then. It has added new weapons systems, better computers, and more accurate radar. The plane's primary function has never changed, though. It remains one of the most reliable bombers in U.S. Air Force service.

WEAPONS AND FEATURES

The B-52 is a huge plane. It can carry up to 70,000 pounds (32,000 kilograms) of weaponry. It can drop unguided "gravity" bombs, laser-guided bombs, **cruise missiles**, and more. The B-52 can also carry nuclear weapons.

The GBU-28 is one of the B-52's most effective bombs. It is a laser-guided bomb. Computers guide it to a target marked by a laser beam. The AGM-129 Advanced Cruise Missile (ACM) is another important B-52 weapon. This missile can break through any missile defense system.

★ FAST FACT ★

The B-52 has a 20mm M61 Vulcan cannon. This huge gun can shoot up to 6,000 rounds per minute.

B-52 SPECIFICATIONS:

Primary Function: Heavy bomber

Length: 159 feet, 4 inches (48.5 meters)

Height: 40 feet, 8 inches (12.4 meters)

Weight: 185,000 pounds (83,250 kilograms)

Wingspan: 185 feet (56.4 meters)

Speed: 650 miles (1,050 kilometers) per hour

Ceiling: 50,000 feet (15,000 meters)

Payload: 70,000 pounds (31,500 kilograms)

Engines: 8 Pratt & Whitney TF33-P-3/103 turbofans

Range: 8,800 miles (14,200 kilometers)

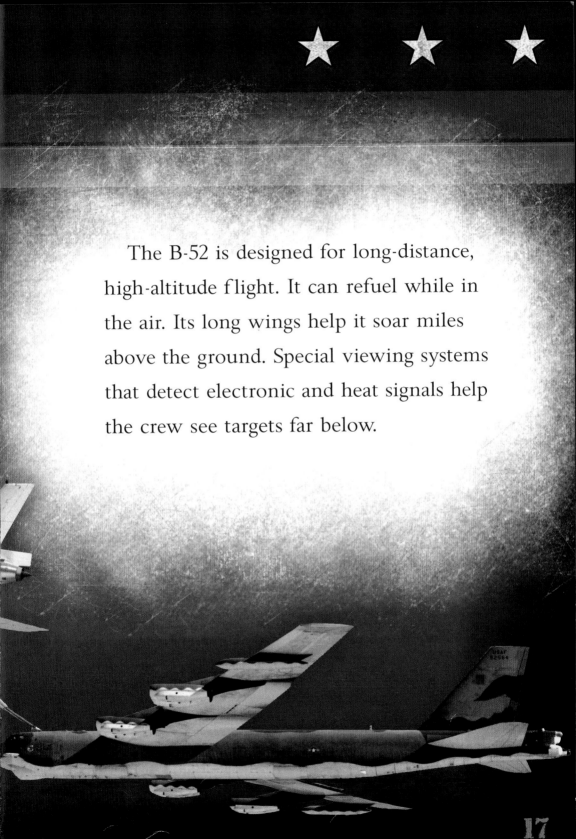

The B-52 is designed for long-distance, high-altitude flight. It can refuel while in the air. Its long wings help it soar miles above the ground. Special viewing systems that detect electronic and heat signals help the crew see targets far below.

B-52 MISSIONS

A B-52 crew can destroy just about any target, day or night. At night, pilots use special **night-vision goggles (NVGs)** to help them see.

A B-52 crew has five members. The
commander is in charge of the crew and gives
the order to deploy weapons. The pilot flies the
plane with the help of the **navigator**. The **radar
navigator** operates the plane's advanced radar
system and helps lock onto targets.

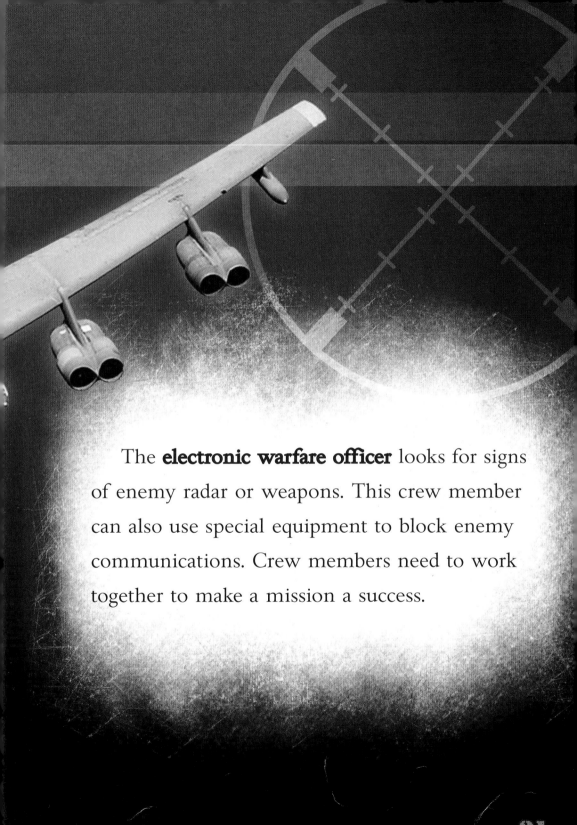

The **electronic warfare officer** looks for signs of enemy radar or weapons. This crew member can also use special equipment to block enemy communications. Crew members need to work together to make a mission a success.

GLOSSARY

altitude—the distance above sea level

commander—the crew member in charge of a B-52

cruise missile—a guided missile that carries explosives and has its own engine

electronic warfare officer—the crew member who operates communication-jamming equipment and looks for enemy radar and weapons signals

laser-guided bomb (LGB)—an explosive that locks onto a target that has been marked with a laser

mission—a military task

navigator—the crew member in charge of assisting the pilot with directions and helping plot a course

night-vision goggles—a special set of glasses that help a user see at night

radar—a sensor system that uses radio waves to locate objects in the air

radar navigator—the B-52 crew member in charge of operating the plane's radar system

TO LEARN MORE

AT THE LIBRARY

Braulick, Carrie A. *U.S. Air Force Bombers*. Mankato, Minn.: Capstone, 2006.

Green, Michael. *Heavy Bombers: The B-52 Stratofortresses*. Mankato, Minn.: Capstone, 2008.

Zobel, Derek. *United States Air Force*. Minneapolis, Minn.: Bellwether, 2008.

ON THE WEB

Learning more about military machines is as easy as 1, 2, 3.

1. Go to www.factsurfer.com.

2. Enter "military machines" into the search box.

3. Click the "Surf" button and you will see a list of related Web sites.

With factsurfer.com, finding more information is just a click away.

INDEX